TO:

FROM:

THE 10 ST🗨RIES

GREAT
LEADERS TELL

FROM BESTSELLING AUTHOR

PAUL SMITH

simple **truths**®
▶ Small books. **BIG IMPACT.**

IGNITE READS
spark impact in just one hour

Internal images © page vi, Jacobs Stock Photography/Getty Images; page xv, Morsa Images/Getty Images; page 10, Ezra Bailey/Getty Images; page 48, Yuri_Arcurs/Getty Images; page 65, JGalione/Getty Images; page 66, Martin Steinthaler/Getty Images; page 75, Astrakan Images/Getty Images; page 102, blackred/Getty Images

Internal images on pages pages xii, xvi, 4, 8, 12, 16, 20, 24, 29, 30, 34, 39, 40, 46, 50, 57, 58, 72, 76, 83, 86, 90, 94, and 106 have been provided by Pexels, Pixabay, and Unsplash; these images are licensed under CC0 Creative Commons and have been released by the author for public use.

Published by Simple Truths, an imprint of Sourcebooks
P.O. Box 4410, Naperville, Illinois 60567-4410
(630) 961-3900
sourcebooks.com

Printed and bound in China.
OGP 10 9 8 7 6 5 4 3 2 1

To my grandfather, Floyd "Ping" Smith

(1901–1995)

A leader in the American dairy industry

whose career spanned eight decades and

who always had a great story

CONTENTS

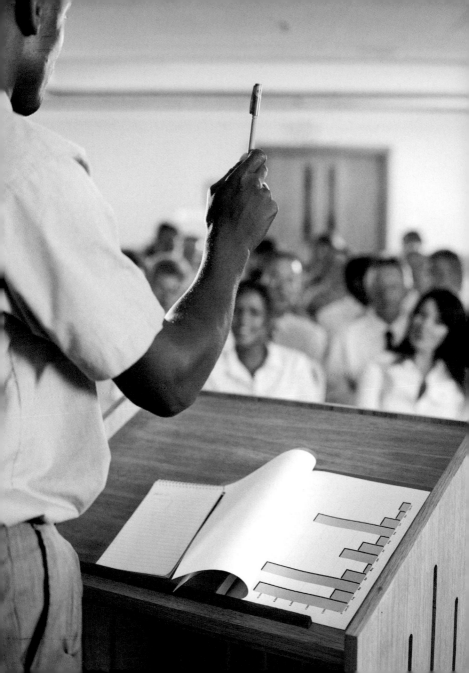

Introduction

Every great leader is a great storyteller. And the first and most important part of being a great storyteller is knowing what stories to tell.

Ironically, journalists and publishers are typically interested in producing content on *how* to craft leadership stories: the structure of the story, emotional elements, the right level of detail, how long they should be, etc. But when I work with executives—actual leaders working in organizations—those aren't the first questions they ask. The first question they typically ask is "*What* stories do I need to tell?"

The reason I side with the executives on what's of foremost importance is that if you tell the right story but butcher the delivery, your audience will forgive you. You're not a novelist or a professional speaker. You're a leader.

But if you tell your people a boring, irrelevant story, even if you deliver it in a way that would make a Shakespearean actor proud, your audience will never forgive you for wasting their time.

What stories you tell is more important than how you tell them.

Will you be more effective as a leader if you learn how to craft more compelling stories? Of course. And I spend most of my professional time teaching leaders how to do exactly that. But the best leaders start by choosing the right stories to tell.

So, my purpose in writing this book is to give leaders of any size or type of organization ten of the most important stories they need to tell, plus a running start at how to find their own.

But before we get to the stories, let me address three brief topics about the list.

First, notice that the title of this book isn't *The 10 Speeches Great Leaders Make*, or *10* Presentations *Great Leaders Give*, or even *10* Ideas *Great Leaders Share*. It's *The 10* Stories *Great Leaders Tell*.

And by *story* I don't mean just a list of the talking points or the message track an executive should have for each topic. I literally mean a narrative about something that happened to someone. As such, it will include a time, a place, and a main character. That main character will have a goal, and there will probably be an obstacle getting in the way of that goal—a villain, if you will. And there will be events that transpire along the way that hopefully resolve themselves in the end. In other words, this isn't just a list of ten topics leaders need to have an articulated opinion on—although they certainly should. It's a list of actual stories they need to tell.

Second, why is it important that these ideas be addressed in the form of stories and not just a set of slides or bullet points in a memo?

Of course, you *should* have a clear, outlined set of ideas for each of these ten topics. And if you're a good leader, you already do. But my purpose in helping you develop *stories* for these topics is that stories are uniquely effective at helping leaders get ideas across in a way that will move people to action. Volumes have been written on why storytelling is so effective. But I'll summarize my top six reasons below. Stories are:

1. **Aids to decision-making.** Research tells us that human beings typically make subconscious, emotional, often irrational decisions in one place in their brain and then rationalize those decisions after the fact in a conscious, logical part of the brain. Facts, data, and arguments only appeal to the rational part of the brain. Stories connect with both.

2 **Timeless.** Storytelling is the oldest form of communication known to man. We've been telling stories since we've been drawing pictures on cave walls. It's not a leadership fad that will ever go out of practice.

3 **Demographic-proof.** Working with hundreds of companies in dozens of countries around the world, I've yet to meet a demographic profile of people who are immune to the effects of a great story.

4 **More memorable.** Studies have shown that facts are more likely to be remembered if they're embedded in a story than if they're just given to people in a list. And you can prove that to yourself while reading this book. By the time you've finished the second chapter, you know that you'll have probably forgotten this list of six reasons storytelling works. But once you've read the stories in each chapter, you'll know just as firmly that you won't soon forget any of them.

5   **Contagious.** Write a good memo and it will stay in email inboxes and file drawers. But tell a good story and it will get forwarded around your world, however big that is.

6   **Inspirational.** Stories inspire. Slides don't. When's the last time you heard someone say, "OMG! You'll never believe the PowerPoint deck I just flipped through!" But you will hear people say that about a good story.

Third, how did I choose these particular ten stories?

As part of my research, I've conducted over three hundred in-depth, one-on-one interviews with CEOs, leaders, and executives in over twenty-five countries around the world. In my previous books—*Lead with a Story*, *Parenting with a Story*, and *Sell with a Story*—I used that research to outline several dozen of the most useful types of business and personal stories (and provided hundreds of the most compelling examples I came across). How did I settle on these particular ten types of stories out of all those options? Four criteria led me there. I looked for stories that:

1   my executive clients most frequently ask me to help them develop;

2   cover the most important territory of ideas about which a leader should have an opinion and exert some influence in the organization;

3 will be useful to leaders in just about any functional discipline, whether that's general management, marketing, sales, finance, human resources, information technology, research and development, etc.; and

4 won't need to change often. That way you'll get a lot of mileage out of each one and a high return on your time invested in getting them right.

More important, however, than *my* reasons for choosing them is what *you*, as a leader, think of them. And I'm confident that as you scan through the list in the table of contents, you'll conclude it's a list of stories you won't want to go without.

Let's get started.

1

Where We Came From

A Founding Story

Nobody ever quit their job and started their own company for a boring reason.

And that's why you should be telling your company's founding story—it's probably exciting. It's certainly more exciting than the reasons most of us take jobs working for someone else, like we need the money or they let you wear jeans on Friday. Sharing the founding story gives employees a chance to be part of something bigger than just their job. It gives them a chance to be part of a larger story.

It also shows them the impetus, passion, and drive behind why the founder started the company to begin with. And in doing so, it'll give your employees that same sense of passion and drive.

But the founding story isn't just useful inside the company. You'll find the founding story useful for several purposes with outside audiences as well. For example:

+ Recruiting—to convince potential employees to want to work there.

+ Sales—to help prospects understand the kind of company you are and why you do what you do.

+ Investor Relations—to help Wall Street analysts, private equity groups, or venture capital firms understand what they're investing in.

Very few investors, prospects, or recruits base their decisions solely on the numbers. They need to believe in your story. And for them to believe in your story, you need to have one.

This is your story—your founding story.

Here's an example:

In the late 1980s, Gary Erickson was living in the San Francisco Bay Area trying to hold down two jobs. During the day, he was managing a bicycle seat manufacturing company. But at night, he was pursuing his real passion—running his own bakery: Kali's Sweets & Savories. He'd named the bakery after his grandmother who, along with his mother, had taught him to bake when he was a kid.[ii]

Another passion he'd developed early was a love of the outdoors that he'd gotten largely from his father, Clifford. Rock climbing and bicycle racing had become two of his regular hobbies.

Then one day in 1990, he was out for a 175-mile,

daylong bike ride around the Bay Area with a friend.[iii] And as most bikers do, he'd brought half a dozen energy bars with him to refuel along the route. At the time there was really only one energy bar on the market. So that's all he was eating.

When they got to the top of Mount Hamilton, east of San Jose, they took a break. Gary had already eaten five of his six bars but was still famished and had fifty miles left to go.[iv] He looked at the sixth one in his hand and thought, *No way. I can't do one more. I'd rather starve than eat another one of these.*[v]

If you're familiar with some of those early energy bars, you understand why. They were hard and sticky and took a while to digest. Eat too many of them and they could sit in your stomach like a rock. Plus, they were none too tasty.

As he was coasting back down into San Jose on an empty stomach, Gary was thinking to himself that he had a bakery, and everything they made tasted great. So why did these energy bars—that just about every cyclist and runner were eating—have to be a bitter pill you had to swallow just to perform? That's when Gary had an epiphany. He turned to his friend and said, "You know what? I can make a better energy bar than this!"[vi]

The next day he called his mom and started working on a formula in her kitchen. He wanted to make something that tasted good, with the texture of a cookie, but with healthy, all-natural ingredients instead of the highly processed bars on the market at the time. After six months of trial and error they'd found just the right recipe—with whole oats and real fruit, but no oil, butter, or added sugar.

He'd already named his bakery after a woman in his family. So, when it came time to give the new product a name, he thought he should name it after his father, Clifford, who'd given him his love of the outdoors and adventures in the first place. So he did. And that's when the CLIF Bar was born.

First-year sales were strong and doubled each year, topping $20 million in 1997.[vii] By the year 2000, Quaker Oats was offering to buy the company for $120 million. And in 2010, *Forbes* recognized it as the number one "Breakaway Brand" based on its three-year momentum.[viii] Today, of course, it's one of the most recognized energy bars anywhere.

Now, to understand why this story works as a founding story, compare it to how most founding stories read: "Our founder started the company in 1936 in her basement with $500 and two employees. Today we have over twenty thousand employees, offices all over the world, and last year made the Fortune 500 list for the first time…" It's similar to the final paragraph of the CLIF Bar story. But it's missing the rest, which is the important part. It has the data. But it's missing the story. The story answers *why* questions, not just *what* questions.

The CLIF Bar story works because it explains why Gary Erickson founded the company in the first place. And that reason was a real, human reason. And that's why employees, customers, and investors can see themselves playing a part in the company.

TIPS TO HELP YOU CRAFT YOUR OWN FOUNDING STORY

If you're lucky, somebody's already documented your company's founding story. Find it. Check the company archives. Ask the company historian. Ask the HR department. If you're even luckier, it's well-crafted already. If so, read it a few times and you're done.

More likely, however, is that your founding story either doesn't exist or it's not very good. In that case, you'll have to craft it yourself. If the founder's still alive, ask for an interview. If not, ask someone else who

knows the original story. Ask questions as if you were an investigative journalist. Then keep asking questions until you find yourself wanting to quit your job and start your own damn company. That's how you'll know you've got the story right.

You're looking for the *pivotal moment* that changed everything, like Gary's epiphany on the top of Mount Hamilton. Don't be satisfied with a vague answer about building a business or even saving the world. Find out what that moment was for your founder and craft a story around it. You'll find more advice about putting that story together in the last chapter, "Taking Your Next Steps."

Why We Can't Stay Here

A Case-for-Change Story

Much of leadership is managing change. If nothing needed changing, we wouldn't need so many smart leaders running companies. They'd all be on autopilot.

But human beings are creatures of habit. And that's a problem. Change means letting go of comfortable habits and familiar routines. And that creates fear, uncertainty, and doubt: "Should I make this change? Can we do it? What if I fail?"

As a result, change is hard work. And that's why convincing people to change is hard work. Fortunately, storytelling is one of the best change agents leaders have at their disposal.

In that effort, the first challenge a leader faces is typically to convince the organization that change is necessary. It answers the question, "Why should I make this change?" The best story, then, will be a story about whoever stands to benefit most from the change.

Here's an example:

In February 2015, National Public Radio aired a story about Joey, a ten-year-old boy in Gainesville, Florida, suffering from a rare form of kidney cancer.[ix] When Joey was diagnosed in March 2013, the cancer had already spread to his abdomen, chest, and neck. He went through two surgeries and five rounds of oral and intravenous chemotherapy, none of which worked for more than a month or two. Eventually, he'd exhausted all the available treatments.

So, his mother, Kathy Liu, tried to get treatments that weren't available. She heard several new immunotherapy treatments were in clinical trials, but none of the trials were accepting children. Those cancers are rare in children and it complicates the testing to include them.

Kathy petitioned the pharmaceutical companies for what's called a compassionate use of the latest experimental drugs. Despite receiving seventeen thousand signatures on her petition, Joey wasn't approved.[x] His condition continued to deteriorate, and he was losing weight. He was down to forty-four pounds.

By mid-2014, with no remaining treatment options, the doctors told Kathy to take Joey home and enjoy their remaining time together.

Kathy was desperate.

"We can't just *go home*," she said. "For us, that means giving up."

Then, in September, the FDA approved Keytruda, created by Merck, the first in the new class of immunotherapy drugs called PD-1 inhibitors. Despite being approved for use, his doctors were hesitant to try the new drug on Joey because it wasn't clinically tested on children.

Kathy called doctors across the country to find one willing to try. Dr. Jim Geller, an oncologist at Cincinnati Children's Hospital, answered that call.

So, Kathy, her husband Luke, their three-year-old David, and Joey all packed their things in Florida and moved to Cincinnati.

Joey got the first injection of Keytruda on October 14, over a year and a half after being diagnosed. The tumors in his neck shrank significantly. And the ones in the rest of his body stabilized. Keytruda was working!

Less than a month later, the day before Thanksgiving, Joey died.

It turns out, Joey was just too weak when the treatment started, and the cancer had an eighteen-month head start.

Kathy told the NPR reporter, "If Joey could [have gotten] this drug last year, even just a couple of months earlier, maybe it [would have been] a different story."

Kathy lost Joey that day. But she hasn't given up her fight. Today, she runs a foundation called Joey's Wings (joeywings.org) that raises awareness and money specifically for pediatric cancer research.

When that story aired on NPR, one of the people who heard it worked at a company that had just retained me as a storytelling coach. The industry they worked in produced lifesaving products but took a notoriously long time to get them to market— sometimes a decade or more.

So, like most of their competitors, one of the things they were working on was how to get products to market faster. But changing a complex, decade-long process is hard work. The motivation to earn profits faster didn't seem sufficient to move the organization to make the radical changes necessary. My job was to help them develop a case-for-change story.

When one of the participants in my workshop shared NPR's story of Kathy and Joey, it immediately became the basis for our story—our case for change.

Think about that. Keytruda wasn't their product. And Joey wasn't their customer. But it did become their story—or at least a fictionalized version of it. Because they knew the same thing was surely happening with the lifesaving products they were working on. And having a human reason to do all this hard work was a more effective motivator than higher profits and a growing stock price.

TIPS TO HELP YOU CRAFT YOUR OWN CASE-FOR-CHANGE STORY

Start by asking yourself: "Who stands to benefit from this change?" Surely, it's good for someone or something your audience cares about, or it wouldn't be a priority for the company.

Once you know who that is, talk to them and ask these kinds of questions:

+ What's your life or work like today (prior to making this change)?

+ What problems or frustrations do you experience?

+ How would your life or work be different once we implement this change?

+ What are the tangible ways you'll know the change is working?

Sure, not everyone will have a story as compelling as Kathy Liu's because not everyone's job is curing cancer. But whatever it is that you and your company are trying to do with this change will surely benefit someone. The point is, a story about the human impact of the change, whether that's a benefit to the employees who have to go through the change or to your customers or to the community, will likely be more compelling than just telling people how much money it'll save.

Craft your own Kathy Liu story. That will be your personal case for change.

Where We're Going

A Vision Story

A vision is a picture of the future so compelling people want to go there with you.

Unfortunately, what passes for a vision today has been tainted by the well-intended but misguided output of off-site meetings and expensive consultants.[xi] The problem is exacerbated by the misperception that the only way to be memorable is to be ridiculously brief. And that's why we've ended up with what amounts to vision sentences or, worse, vision phrases instead of vision stories.

For example, after weeks of deliberation, one organization I was part of articulated their five-year vision—to much fanfare—with the following five words: "40 and 5 in 5." What that meant was that we wanted to reach $40 billion in sales and add five points to our market share over the next five years. Or, maybe it was to reach a 40 percent market share and add $5 billion in sales in five years. I can't really remember. And even when I could, those arbitrary goals did very little to motivate me to do anything differently. And that's the point. Brief doesn't equal memorable, and it certainly doesn't equal meaningful.

Here's a better way I stumbled across: In 2002, I'd been assigned to lead a group of forecasters whose job was to predict the future sales of new products where I worked. But, since you can never predict the future perfectly, they knew their prediction would be wrong. They just didn't know if it would be too high or too low, and by how much. To make matters worse, they were often undertrained and had forecasting models that were overly complicated, poorly documented, and based on outmoded data.

My job was to lead them through whatever changes were needed to fix all that. But the solution wasn't something I could just do for them. It would require a lot of work on their part. My challenge was to lay out a vision and, hopefully, inspire enough of them to do the hard work necessary to get there. But instead of a vision phrase or a vision sentence or even a vision statement, I wrote them a vision story.

It started out like this:

Below is a picture of the future I'd like to help you create. It's my vision of what a day in the life of a sales forecaster could be in the near future. Some of you may feel you're already pretty close to this, and some may feel infinitely far away. Either way, I want to make this a vision we all share—either by adding

your ideas to it or embracing it as is. Let me know what you think.

In the subject line of the email, I wrote "The Vision: A Day in the Life of a Sales Forecaster." The story it contained introduced "Sherri, a sales fore-caster two years in the future." The story simply followed Sherri through a single day in her work life—what she did and the meetings she attended.

And for the people reading it, it was clear how different her experience was from what they experienced day-to-day:

- ▸ The story followed Sherri to meetings that she previously wouldn't have been invited to because her opinion wasn't valued as highly as it was now.

- ▸ Instead of feeling uncertain when answering questions from her business partners, she felt confident, because she'd been more properly trained and her models were updated with the most recent data.

- ▸ Instead of fumbling around in her forecast model trying to figure out how it worked and troubleshooting issues, she simply opened her new instruction manual and followed the instructions. Besides, the new model was a lot easier to figure out because it was so much simpler than the old one.

As the story continued, it became clear that she experienced none of the typical frustrations a forecaster would be familiar with.

The story closed at the end of the day when Sherri was walking out of a meeting. Two people thanked her for her great ideas and said that they liked this new leadership role the forecasters seemed to be playing in the business. The final words of the story read, "She hadn't realized it before now, but she actually liked her job. It was more fun to come to work when you know what you're doing and you're having a big impact on results."

The first response I got to the email was, "Wow! I want that to be my story two years from now. I'm in!" After a dozen or so more responses like that, I knew I'd stumbled onto something right with the story.

TIPS TO HELP YOU CRAFT YOUR OWN VISION STORY

+ Decide who your audience is. Who are you writing the vision story for? Is it for management? The rank and file? Your investors? It might be several audiences, in which case you might need several vision stories. But for most companies, the goal of the vision is to inspire the broad set of employees.

+ Who or what will benefit most if your vision is achieved? Is it the employees? Stockholders? Customers? The environment? The community?

+ Choose a fictional character either from the group your audience is in or the group that stands to benefit from the vision. Ideally, they're both the same group. But they don't have to be, as long as your audience cares about the group that will benefit. This will be the main character of your vision story. EXPAND

+ Sketch out what a typical day is like for them after your vision has been achieved.

+ Make sure to include the type of activities that are both important to your audience and heavily impacted by having achieved the vision.

> *What's better about working at a company that's winning in the marketplace (if that's your goal)? Will employees be prouder to work there? Perhaps show your main character reading a flattering article about your company in Fortune.*

> *What's better about working at a company that's growing sales and profits faster than ever before (if that's your goal)? Will that mean bigger*

bonuses at the end of the year? Will it open up new job opportunities for your employees or create more challenging work? Show that in the story.

+ Conclude with a summation of how your main character feels about the world he or she is living and working in now compared to the way things were before.

STORY

4

How We're Going to Get There

A Strategy Story

Strategy is how you'll get from where you are now to where you want to be. In other words, strategy is a journey. And what better way to describe a journey than a story?

Your strategy story will be informed by the three stories that preceded this one: where you started (founding), why you can't stay there (case for change), and where you want to go (vision). And it represents your choices for what you will do (and won't do) in order to get there.

While some companies share their strategy outside the company (to woo investors, for example) most share it internally to help employees understand and embrace the work they have to do. But let's face it, most company strategy documents are a boring read at best, and incomprehensible management-speak at worst. A story makes the complex strategy simple and accessible to the entire company.

Here's a creative case in point: The cough/cold industry is obviously a seasonal business. The overwhelming majority of cold medicines, cough syrups, decongestants, and facial tissues are sold in either the winter cold season or spring allergy season. And like many other businesses, there's usually one dominant brand in each of those categories, and then distant second- and third-place brands.

One year, all the employees at one of those second-place brands arrived at work to find something unexpected on their desks—a copy of what looked like an article from the *Wall Street Journal*. Except it wasn't really a *Journal* article. It was just a memo designed to look like one. Oddly, the date at the top was six years into the future. And the byline identified the author as one of the executives who worked in their business unit. So, while nobody was fooled, it was all strange enough to convince everyone to read it. The title was "How David Beat Goliath."

Here's a synopsis of what it said:

Vivek grew up in Mumbai playing soccer.[xii] **So, when he moved to the United States and saw his first basketball game, he was puzzled. The court is 94 feet long. But each team only actively defends the 24 feet in front of their goal. The offense lazily walks the other 70 feet dribbling the ball uncontested. That would never happen in soccer.**

Then Vivek's twelve-year-old daughter signed up to play basketball on a new team that consisted

of, as Vivek described them, "a bunch of blonde girls from Menlo Park" who had never played the game and had no coach. Vivek knew they had very little chance of winning a game even with a coach, and none without. So, he volunteered.

They ended up in the national championships.

How? They changed the game. Instead of conventional basketball, Vivek's girls ran a full-court press, every game, all the time. His girls played 94 feet all season long.

Why did it work? It worked because when you're the underdog, letting your opponent play the game they trained for is a sure path to defeat. Vivek's opponents had very little practice against a full-court press. And when they did get the ball within 24 feet to make a play, they were too exhausted to execute it.

And that's exactly what this second-tier brand in the cough/cold category did that year. They took plays right out of Vivek's playbook. Instead of only running advertisements during cold and allergy season, they started advertising twelve months a year. The ground they gained in off-peak time gave them a head start the next peak season.

Their next unconventional move was to stop marketing their brand as only good for colds and allergies. For example, you can use facial tissues to remove makeup or wipe away tears, not just blow your nose. And while most brands market their products exclusively to women (who still make about 80 percent of the purchase decisions), they started advertising to men also. Those new uses and new buyers grew their market share even more.

But they didn't stop with just marketing changes. They started innovating with their product as well: Self-dosing lids, designer boxes, and packaging so soft you could curl up with it in bed when you're sick. Each new idea brought new sales.

The memo went on to describe equally radical changes the brand had made to retail shelf strategies, promotional strategies, and new places to use the product nobody had ever thought of before. The final line of the article said that after five years of executing these strategies, this distant little second-place brand overtook the dominant brand in market share for the first time in its fifty-year history. "David 37%. Goliath 36%."

At the bottom of the article was a handwritten note that said, "Thanks for everything you did to achieve these amazing results!—the boss."

Yes, because it was dated in the future you could consider this a vision story. But make no mistake, this was a strategy story. It explained each piece of the brand's strategy and why each one would work, using layman's terms, a brilliant analogy, and an inspiring story. By the afternoon, people all over the office had pinned that article to their cubicle walls. And for weeks, the author was stopped in the hallway by people he'd never met before thanking him for writing such an inspiring article and for explaining the strategy in a way they could understand, appreciate, and most importantly, execute.

A well-crafted strategy story can do the same for you.

TIPS TO HELP YOU CRAFT YOUR OWN STRATEGY STORY

To try this particular execution:

+ Pick a date in the future by which your strategy should have worked.

+ Write what amounts to a newspaper or magazine article looking back at your success.

+ Include the metrics of your success (revenues, profits, market share, etc.).

+ Describe each component of your strategy in terms of how it played out, and how it impacted your business results versus your competitors.

+ You certainly don't need to use a sports analogy

for your business strategy. But if your audience can relate to the one you choose, it can definitely help. Both are highly competitive endeavors, there are winners and losers, and a good strategy can be the difference between which one you are.

+ It also doesn't have to be a story looking back from the future. It can be a hypothetical story delivered in present tense. To do that, simply begin your story with the words, "Imagine this..."

What We Believe

A Corporate-Values Story

Every company has them—*corporate-values statements*. Sometimes they're called *company values and principles* or simply *what we believe*.

But values are only words on a piece of paper until they're tested. That is, until someone is put in a difficult position of choosing between doing the hard right or the easy wrong. The easy wrong is usually more attractive in the short term: it's more profitable, more convenient, helps you avoid an embarrassment, or just makes you look good.

That's why stories are uniquely called for when trying to establish values in an organization. Only a story can convey the uncomfortable or awkward predicament required to truly define a value. Sharing those stories with your organization will show them what happens when you actually act on your values.

Here's an example:

Almost everyone reading this will be familiar with Sam Walton, the retailer who founded Walmart stores in 1962 in Arkansas. But fewer will be familiar with Florence Butt, the woman who founded H. E. Butt (H-E-B) grocery stores in San Antonio, Texas, in 1905.

For much of the twentieth century, H-E-B was the largest grocery store chain in Texas. That is, until Walmart came along. Within two decades of opening, Walmart had overtaken H-E-B as the leading grocery retailer in Texas.

It would be fair to say, then, that Sam Walton and Charles Butt (H-E-B's CEO and grandson of the founder) were fierce competitors. That fact makes the following tale all the more impressive, as recounted by John Pepper in his book, *What Really Matters*.[xiii]

In an effort to learn from his now-larger competitor, Charles Butt once asked Sam Walton if he could bring his leadership team to Walmart's headquarters on a learning mission. Sam said that he wasn't sure if he could help, but he'd be happy to try.

On the scheduled day, Charles Butt and his senior executives arrived in Arkansas and met Sam at one of his local stores. When Charles walked in, he could see Sam at the end of a long aisle talking to a customer. Not one to waste time, Charles walked up the aisle with his team. When Sam saw them, he said, "Charles, I'll be with you in a moment. I'm talking to this young woman." He was trying to sell her an ironing board cover.

After a few more minutes of conversation, the

woman put the ironing board cover in her cart and pushed off toward the register. Sam turned to Charles and asked him with great seriousness, "Charles, do you know how many worn-out ironing board covers there are in this country? We're going to sell a million this month!"

Charles commented later that he had no doubt Walmart would sell those million ironing board covers. And in fact, it did.

Now, imagine you're an employee at Walmart today, and your boss told you that story. What lessons about company values could you learn? I've shared that story and asked that question to thousands of participants in training classes over the past six years. I never get fewer than ten solid answers. Here are the most popular five:

1 **Other retailers are our competitors, not our enemies.** We work in the same industry serving the

same customers. If we can help each other serve those customers without giving away our competitive secrets, we should.

2 **The customer is number one.** When approached by H-E-B's CEO, who he'd invited to fly hundreds of miles to meet with him, Sam Walton chose to make the CEO wait while he helped a customer.

3 **Understanding the customer's wants and needs is important.** Why do you think Sam knew there were so many worn-out ironing board covers in the country? He asked.

4 **Persistence pays off.** Valuing persistence means you don't give up until you've helped the customer find what they're looking for. Sam didn't quit until the woman was satisfied with her choice and put the ironing board cover in her cart.

5   **Passion wins**. Out of the billions of dollars of merchandise Walmart sells every year, Sam had set a goal specifically for how many ironing board covers he wanted to sell (a million this month), and he was clearly excited by the challenge. Passion is contagious. Spread it and you'll be amazed what you can accomplish.

A story like this can convey a number of values far better than a corporate-values statement.

TIPS TO HELP YOU CRAFT YOUR OWN VALUES STORY

+ Find your company values statement. (It's probably hidden in a dusty file drawer somewhere.)

+ Go through each item on the list and ask questions like these:

  ▸ *When have I seen someone's behavior exemplify this value? What happened and how did it reflect on that person and the company?*

  ▸ *When have I seen someone's behavior show the opposite character? What happened and what were the negative ramifications for that person and the company?*

▸ *When have I or someone else at this company found themselves:*

◆ struggling to decide what the right thing to do was?

◆ making a promise and had trouble keeping it?

◆ getting out the policy manual or asking HR before making a tough decision?

◆ being asked to do something they didn't feel comfortable doing?

◆ acting in a way that would make the company's founder proud?

◆ feeling conflicted about two separate values on the list?

Pick the situation that best illustrates the value or values most important to you personally. Build a story around that moment. Share it and ask people what values they learn from it before telling them what you learned from it. Chances are they'll learn the same thing you did.

Who We Serve

A Customer Story

Spy novelist John Le Carré once observed, "A desk is a dangerous place from which to view the world." If the only customer information used in your organization comes from dry PowerPoint presentations and impersonal statistical data, you probably don't understand your customer any better than you understand your own medical charts.

There's no substitute for getting out of the office

and meeting your customer face-to-face. But since not everyone in the company can do that as often as they should, you, as a leader, should be telling the stories of the people who did—especially the truly enlightening ones.

Here's an example:

In 1993, Rohini was a new marketing manager for a brand of disposable feminine protection pads in India. She was on a three-day visit to the southern Indian city of Chennai to conduct in-home research. Her goal was to find out what was driving low-income women to buy her expensive brand of disposable pads when they had been using cheap, reusable cloth pads during their menstrual period.

When she arrived at her first interview, the woman of the house smiled and invited Rohini to sit on one of the only two metal folding chairs in the room. Rohini took in her surroundings: It was a two-room dwelling, small kitchen alcove, no TV, no refrigerator, and no air-conditioning. Behind the door, on two nails, hung a man's shirt, trousers, and a blue-checked linen towel. And on the table under the window, precisely stacked, were a pile of school exercise books, primly covered in the regulation brown paper.

The woman looked older than her years, and tired. Rohini was intensely conscious that she was interrupting her quiet time of the day, when her children were away at school and her husband was at work. She described their conversation this way:

Early on in the discussion, it became clear that she wasn't using our product herself. She was buying it for her eighth-grade daughter, who had been using cloth. I asked her why she'd started spending money on it if her daughter had already become used to cloth.

"It's because she has to go to school, you see," she replied.

"Well, what did your daughter do about school when she was using cloth?"

"She would go, all right, but she just felt uncomfortable...couldn't concentrate. With these pads, she doesn't feel the wetness, so she feels more comfortable. And she doesn't have to worry about staining."

"But don't you think that it's a bit expensive for you, just to give a comfortable feeling to your daughter once in a while?" I asked.

"Yes, it is expensive, but then she needs to be able to concentrate in school, to get good marks."

So I asked, "Why is that important? After all, presumably you will want to get her married after school, so why are good marks important?"

"I want her to study further after school. I don't want her to get married too early."

"But you yourself got married at the age of sixteen. What's wrong with that?"

She leaned forward and looked me in the eyes as she explained very soberly: "I don't want my daughter to be like me. I want my daughter to be financially independent, to be able to feel comfortable in the outside world. Whether she marries or not will be up to her. She has to study, get good marks, and go to college and then get a job. I don't want her to have two kids by the age of twenty. I live my life through my children; I don't have many aspirations for my own life now. But my daughter must be different from me. And that's why these pads make sense to me."

No doubt Rohini's team wrote a proper, clinical summary of their conclusions and observations on that research trip. But the most effective vehicle she left for helping others understand the customer was the intimate portrait contained in the story about meeting that one woman in Chennai. That story has been circulating around her company for over two decades now and helps new employees understand their consumer to this day. Meanwhile, the statistical summary probably hasn't been seen in twenty-five years.

TIPS TO HELP YOU CRAFT YOUR OWN CUSTOMER STORY

+ Get out of the office and meet your customer face-to-face.

  ▸ *Go on a sales call with the sales team.*

  ▸ *Tag along with the research department on a customer visit.*

  ▸ *Stop a shopper in the aisle at the grocery store when you see them buying your product.*

  ▸ *Whatever you have to do, make it happen.*

+ When you get back, write a story about your experience and what you learned.

+ Ask other leaders about their personal experiences with consumers and customers. Somebody has a great customer story like Rohini's. Find it, and tell that story.

What the hell does that even mean? A mouthful of buzzwords and management-speak rarely clarifies anything.

Right about now, many of you are thinking that some of the time that person confusing everyone is you. And that's one reason you need at least one good story to help explain, in concrete terms, what it is you or your company does for your customers. And that story is just as important to share inside the company as outside the company. It's hard to run a world-class operation when the accounts payables clerks and the whole IT department don't have a visceral understanding of what your company does.

Here's an example that makes it crystal clear:

Ben Koberna is one of the founders of EASIBuy, a company that runs reverse auctions for buyers. That means it finds and convinces several suppliers to participate in a competitive bidding process to supply whatever the client needs at the lowest cost.

And while that short description thoroughly and accurately describes what his company does, it leaves all kinds of questions unanswered. So, when he's talking to a new prospect, he almost always tells the story about one of his very first clients:

"It was a midsize county government in central Florida. They'd been paying $250,000 a year for a contractor to haul away the sludge from their waste-water treatment plant. So, they hired us to do a reverse auction to see if they could save some money.

"We looked around and found several sludge-removal companies that were interested and invited them to a pre-bid meeting so we could explain the process. Well, the guy who had the contract at the time showed up with a lawyer, yelling and scream-ing, and even kicked over a chair! He told us the whole process was illegal and said we were all going to be arrested.

"We eventually got him settled down and a couple of weeks later we started the bidding process. His first bid was $250,000, of course. Then, when more aggressive bids started coming in, he lowered his bid to $240,000, then $200,000, then $150,000. The next bid he put in was for $0. Obviously, that was a mistake. So, we paused the auction and called him on the phone. We explained his mistake and told him we could strike that bid and reset the auction.

"But he told us that wouldn't be necessary. He said, 'I didn't make a mistake. I've been selling that sludge to local farmers for the last twenty years to use as fertilizer. I'll just come pick it up for free.'

"And my client has been saving $250,000 a year ever since."

Ben's story answers a lot of questions his prospects eventually ask, and even some they don't know or are afraid to ask. For example, the story answers questions like "Do I have to find all the vendors to bid?" (Nope. That's our job.) and "How do we explain to them how the process will work?" (You don't. We do that for you in a pre-bid meeting.)

But it also answers this more uncomfortable question: "Will my current supplier get mad at me for doing this?" Because the truth is, in Ben's experience, they will get mad. And most clients worry about that because they've been doing business with these people for years. They know them personally. And nobody wants to upset someone they've known and worked with for a long time.

But, as this story illustrates, it doesn't matter if they get upset, because they won't get mad at the client. They'll get mad at Ben. That's part of what the client is paying for—for EASIBuy to shoulder the brunt of the emotional reaction this kind of a process creates. All the client has to do is save money.

TIPS TO HELP YOU CRAFT YOUR OWN SALES STORY

If you have personal experience working with customers, you might be able to craft this story by yourself. If not, you'll probably need to enlist the help of someone in the sales department. They may even have stories like this they can tell you off the top of their head. Share the EASIBuy story with them as an example of what you're looking for. Then do the following:

+ Choose a client from a typical industry you serve— preferably one with a great experience working with you as a supplier. (You don't have to use the client's real name.)

+ Sketch out a brief outline of events that led up to them needing your product or services. It must be a specific instance.

+ List the main steps of what your company did for them.

+ Explain the outcome in terms of how it benefited the customer or consumer.

8

How We're Different from Our Competitors

A Marketing Story

As any first-year MBA student can attest, marketing is largely about differentiation. It communicates how your product or service is different from your many competitors. And that's important because, as I learned from interviewing procurement managers at dozens of companies, competitors in many industries are so similar that it's difficult for even professional buyers to tell them apart.

Marketers use a number of approaches to accomplish that differentiation, from a straightforward list of the distinguishing features and benefits, to branding, customer segmentation, stratified pricing, and many others.

But as a leader, whether you're talking to a prospective customer, the investment community, or just helping the people in your department appreciate why your company's product is better than the competition, your best tool is a story.

For example, Sharad Madison is the CEO of the commercial cleaning company United Building Maintenance. When Sharad is trying to explain how his company is different from his many competitors, he often tells the following story about what he does when he acquires a new client:

When we take over a new contract, we typically have a thirty-day transition period. We take that time to go into the new building in the middle of the night to see how they're cleaning it, to find out if they're properly trained and have the right tools.

For example, we recently took over the contract for the Verizon building in New Jersey. That's a 1.7-million-square-foot property across several buildings. So, we went in and found a guy vacuuming the carpet. It turns out, he was using the same kind of residential-quality vacuum cleaner you probably use at home. Now, those hallways are twelve feet wide and over half a mile long. Can you imagine trying to clean the whole property with the same machine you use at home? It could take a week, and it still wouldn't be very clean. Plus, that vacuum will have to be replaced every few months.

We ordered him a triple-wide, industrial-strength vacuum that'll do the job in less than half the time and last forever.

Then we went to another floor and found someone shampooing those same carpets with a regular walk-behind shampooer. Again, that could take all night just to shampoo that one floor. We put him in a high-speed riding shampooer that could do the job in a fraction of the time with much better results. Plus, it gets the guy off his feet. It's safer for him and means fewer workman's comp issues for me and the client.

Then we got to the offices and started looking at the top of the file cabinets. You could see half-moons swiped out on top of them. I know exactly why that happens. Those cabinets were five and a half feet tall and several of the people cleaning them were shorter than that. So, it's not that they're lazy. They just couldn't reach high enough to clean all the way to the back.

We showed them what that looks like to the client and explained that the half-moon is actually worse than not cleaning it at all, since it's the

contrast that makes it look dirty. And then we gave them all plastic extension wands so they could reach all the way to the back.

Now, compare that story to how Sharad might explain his points of differentiation if he was using the more typical "features and benefits" type of marketing language. It would sound something like this: "What makes us different is that we equip our cleaners with triple-wide, industrial-strength vacuum cleaners, high-speed riding shampooers, and extension wands for dusting."

And that's true. Those are the facts. But the story is far more compelling because, with the story, listeners can see in their minds' eyes all of those pieces of equipment in use. They can see the guy going from the cheap vacuum cleaner to the triple-wide one. They can picture the guy riding around on the shampooer like the Zamboni driver on an ice-skating rink. And they can see very clearly someone

easily cleaning all the way to the back of a tall, dusty cabinet with a plastic extension wand.

Plus, the story makes it obvious that Sharad and his management team care enough to get up in the middle of the night to go walk those floors and see how to make improvements. Just mentioning that you check up on things on-site isn't nearly as convincing as a story that proves you did.

TIPS TO HELP YOU CRAFT YOUR OWN MARKETING STORY

Ask the following questions. You might need to get input from the sales, marketing, or market research departments to find good answers.

+ Think of a time that you (or someone else) used one of your competitor's products or services and had a bad experience. What was that experience like, and how does it differ from an experience with your product?

+ Think of some of the most positive customer-success stories at your company. What was so fabulous about them that isn't likely to happen with competing products?

+ My favorite: Talk to some of your customers who

used to use your competitors' products but have switched to yours. What about their experience made them switch? And what has been their experience now with your product?

Choose one of those experiences and craft a story around it that illustrates the difference between your product or service and your competitor's. It could simply be two stories told one after the other: a bad customer experience with your competitor's product, and a good customer experience with your product.

Why I Lead the Way I Do

A Leadership-Philosophy Story

I've always been impressed with people forward-thinking enough to write down their own leadership philosophy. But I'm rarely impressed with what that philosophy is. It's usually just a bunch of trite, worn-out platitudes and meaningless buzzwords that sound something like this:

> **My leadership philosophy is to synergistically leverage my organization's unique capabilities**

> **and value-added activities to drive employee engagement, outside-the-box thinking, and ultimately maximize value creation for our shareholders, employees, and customers.**

It's so vague and impersonal I could have taken any of the dozens I've been handed in the past and switched the names at the top and it wouldn't have made me think any differently about the people who wrote them. They were that meaningless.

This isn't to say that helping people in your organization understand your leadership philosophy isn't important. It's just that a bunch of buzzwords on a page could never adequately articulate the subtle, human, and complex nature of leadership. The only thing capable of that kind of finesse is a story. Or, more likely, several stories. But let's start with one:

> **In 1995, Mike Figliuolo was a tank platoon leader in the U.S. Army in charge of fifteen soldiers who**

manned four M1A1 main battle tanks. In April of that year, his platoon was preparing to conduct a field training exercise at the National Training Center in Fort Irwin, California. You might call it war games, complete with real tanks and a real field, but with simulated weapons. It was basically a game of laser tag with tanks. The tanks were equipped with laser sensors on the side as well as sirens and an emergency vehicle "whoopie" light on top that identified a tank that had been shot.

The exercise required them to charge ten miles to the center of a five-mile-wide battlefield to engage and destroy (virtually) the opposing force.

As fate would have it, Mike was commanding the lead tank of the lead platoon of the lead company of the lead battalion in the brigade combat team. So, he would literally be in the first tank among four hundred vehicles going into battle, in a wedge formation, on his side of the field.

During the planning phase, Mike and his

commanding officer assessed the map of the field. There were several hills, and they decided on one particular pass between them that would be the safest and fastest route.

When the exercise started, Mike's tank sped toward the enemy as planned. But a battlefield rarely looks like it does on a map, especially when you're looking at it through the tiny opening in the hatch while moving 40 miles per hour and being shot at.

When they approached the hills, Mike wasn't sure which way to go. So, he had a decision to make. Option one: he could stop the tank, pull out the map, and figure out the right way to go. But the tanks were in a tight formation, and all of them would have had to stop along with him. That would leave them all sitting in the open, subject to enemy fire.

Option two: he could make an educated guess, keep moving forward, and take his chances.

Mike chose option two.

He yelled out, "Driver, go left! Take the left pass!"

Less than a minute after his tank turned left, his whoopie light and siren told Mike that he'd made the wrong choice. His tank and crew were now dead and disabled.

A few seconds later, the light on his wingman's tank started to flash, followed by the light on the third tank.

But the fourth tank, and the other 396 vehicles in the battalion, saw what happened and realized it was the wrong decision. All of them headed right, flooded through the correct pass, and defeated the opposing battalion on the other side.

It was an important lesson for Mike. It taught him the value of decisiveness. In war, and in business, it's often better to make the wrong decision quickly than to make the right decision slowly. Bad decisions usually become evident before too long and can be corrected. But indecision can cost you the battle because while you're studying the problem your opponents are still moving forward.

That experience indelibly influenced Mike's personal leadership philosophy which, not surprisingly, is very decisive. Today, as the founder and managing director of the leadership training firm *thought***LEADERS**, LLC, Mike makes well-informed decisions. But he doesn't fall victim to the analysis paralysis that troubles so many organizations today. By comparison, his decisions can seem quick. But he also has a higher tolerance for mistakes than many other leaders do, as long as people learn from those mistakes. Sharing his story of that field training exercise is one way he helps his trainers, partners, and clients expect that kind of leadership behavior from him when it happens, and plan accordingly.

A story like that of your own can do the same for you.

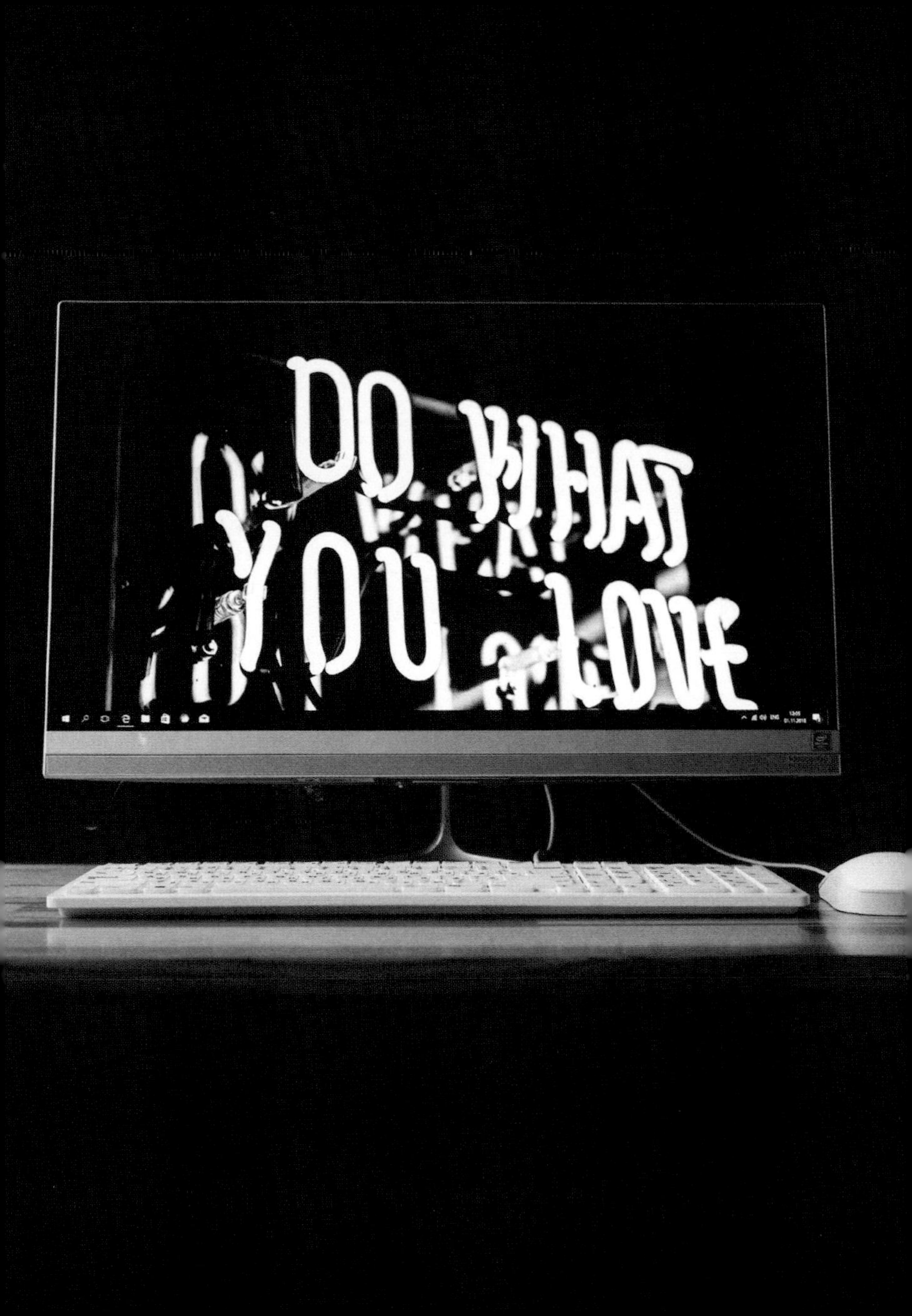
DO WHAT
YOU LOVE

TIPS TO HELP YOU CRAFT YOUR OWN LEADERSHIP-PHILOSOPHY STORY

To help find personally defining moments like this in your life as a leader, ask yourself these questions:

+ What was your biggest leadership mistake and what did you learn from it?

+ What leadership decision are you most proud of and why?

+ What leader do you most admire and what was the moment you realized you did?

+ What guidelines do you operate by at work and why?

+ What one or two principles are you least willing to sacrifice to achieve your goals and why?

+ If you could travel back in time, what one piece of advice would you give your younger self when you were just starting out?

Pick one of the moments you thought of from that list of questions and build a story around it. Use the tools in the last chapter to help.[1]

---

1   To learn more about crafting your own personal leadership philosophy defined by a set of stories like this, check out Mike Figliuolo's book *One Piece of Paper: The Simple Approach to Powerful, Personal Leadership.*

STORY

10

Why You Should Want To Work Here

A Recruiting Story

If you've ever been to a job fair, you've seen this yourself. Go up to any of the booths and ask the recruiter why you should want to work at their company. I can tell you the answers you'll get: competitive pay and benefits, challenging jobs, a chance to work with smart people, and great opportunities for advancement. And if the job fair is in Silicon Valley, you'll also hear about the free lunch and foosball table in the break room.

Then, go to the next booth and ask the same question.

Right. You'll get the same answer. And that's why you need a recruiting story. After hearing about the salary and other basics, human beings need a human reason to make a decision as important as what company to work for. And that means these stories will work just as well at convincing current employees to stay as it does getting new recruits to join.

That story could help them understand what it's really like to work there. It could illustrate a unique and creative way someone made the decision to take the job. Or it could be a surprising reason why someone chose to stay working at your company instead of quitting like they'd planned.

No matter which it is, it's something that you, as a leader, can give them that's not in the brochure.

Here's an example:

In the spring of 1993, I was finishing my MBA at the Wharton School at the University of Pennsylvania. I'd spent much of the previous semester in job interviews, and was trying to decide what career path to follow and what company to join. I was fortunate that the job market was strong that year, so I ended up with multiple offers. And with offers from companies like Johnson & Johnson, Unilever, and Procter & Gamble (P&G), it was going to be a tough decision. All of them offered roughly the same compensation and benefits. Even the career paths and job assignments were remarkably similar. I was stumped.

So, I pulled out the phone book and I called an executive search firm. I told the first person who would talk to me that I didn't need their services—yet. But that I still wanted their advice. I told the guy on the other end of the line my situation: new MBA grad, multiple job offers, etc. I gave him the names of all the companies and the jobs and salaries

I'd been offered. Then I asked him this question: "If I called you five years from now and wanted to move to a new company, which of these companies would you find it easiest to place me from?"

Without hesitating, the guy said, "Procter & Gamble."

I said, "How can you be so sure?"

He said, "Two reasons. First, I place people into and out of all of those companies all the time. After a year, I call them up and ask them how things are going. For the people I place out of P&G into other companies, I consistently hear this complaint: 'It's good here, but the people just aren't as sharp or talented as I was used to working with at P&G.' And I rarely heard that complaint in the other direction."

"And the second reason?" I asked.

He said, "Because P&G is still a promote-from-within company, and none of the others are. That means they only hire people at the entry level. I can

get you a job at any of those other companies any time you want. But if you ever want to work at P&G, you'll have to do it now."

I started my job at P&G in June. And that three-minute phone call with a headhunter was the reason why.

For the next several years, anytime I found myself on the P&G recruiting team headed back to my alma matter to woo the next round of MBA graduates, I brought that story with me. It certainly didn't replace all the flashy PowerPoint presentations and expensive dinner budgets. Nor did it replace the talking points and list of reasons to come work at P&G.

But as we've already discussed, many of the companies recruiting for top talent give the same reasons. Having one more person on the recruiting team repeat the list doesn't help much. But the story was unique, it articulated real points of difference, and it allowed the listener to consider making the same phone call I did, not just take my word for it.

TIPS TO HELP YOU CRAFT YOUR OWN RECRUITING STORY

Ask yourself, and the people you work with, these three questions:

1 What made you want to come to work here?

2 Why do you stay?

3 Have you ever thought about quitting but decided not to? What made you change your mind?

Keep asking until you come across a great story. Not everyone will have one. But somebody will. And that's your recruiting story.

CONCLUSION
Taking Your Next Steps

Congratulations on your journey so far! I'll assume your head is swimming with ideas for your ten stories, and perhaps you've even made good progress on some of them. In this last chapter, I'll offer a few ideas to help you finish that progress and turn those ideas into a final set of ten great leadership stories.

1 The best way to start is to get a copy of *The 10 Stories Great Leaders Tell* Workbook. It has

THE 10 STORIES GREAT LEADERS TELL

everything you need to complete the journey in one place.

2. Your second most important tool is the Story Checklist in the Appendix on page 103 of this book. Here's how to use it:

  a. Use the first column on the right to prioritize your stories. Which ones do you need most urgently, and which ones can wait? Put an A, B, or C next to each one based on its relative importance or urgency.

  b. In the next column, write down the name of the person or event you plan to craft the story about.

  c. Check the box in the last column only after you've finalized the story and you're ready to share it with others. You'll find more advice in steps 4–7 to help you get each story in final shape.

3. Start hunting for stories you don't already have. Start with your A-priority stories. Here's how:

a. Search your own past. Interview yourself to see if you have any great story material lurking in your own memory.

b. Get stories from other people:

    i. Share your Story Checklist with your coworkers, direct reports, bosses, customers, the sales department, marketing, accounting, the warehouse, etc.—anyone who might have a great story to share. You'll be surprised how willing people will be to share their stories when they know you're looking for one.

    ii. Hold a contest and give away a prize for the best story submissions.

    iii. Solicit customer and sales stories on your website. Offer an incentive to share.

4 Make sure your stories answer the following eight questions, preferably in this order.[xv] This is the structure of a well-told business story. It makes sure you provide enough information, but not too much.

And it also makes sure you're putting your ideas in story form. In storytelling, the lesson and recommended action belong at the end, not at the beginning, like it would in a memo or presentation.

#1 Why should your audience listen to your story? (hook)

#2 Where and when did the story take place? (context)

#3 Who is the main character and what did that person want? (context)

#4 What was the problem or opportunity the main character ran into? (challenge)

#5 What did he or she do about it? (conflict or struggle)

#6 How did it turn out in the end? (resolution)

#7 What did you learn from it? (lesson)

#8 What do you think your audience should do now that they've heard it? (recommendation)

5   Last, start telling your stories—in meetings, at lunches, in the hallway, and with your employees, your customers, and your board of directors. Keep

what works and jettison what doesn't. The best way to hone your leadership stories is to start leading with them.

There's a lot more to learn about how to turn good stories into great ones that's beyond the scope of this book. For more guidance on using the eight questions listed previously, plus the use of emotion, surprise, dialog, and details in your stories, see Part II of my book *Sell with a Story.*[xvi]

Need more help? Visit me at leadwithastory.com for training courses and coaching help with your stories.

PHOTO BY LUCAS DEMING

About the Author

Paul Smith is one of the world's leading experts in business storytelling. He's one of *Inc.* magazine's Top 100 Leadership Speakers of 2018, a storytelling coach, and bestselling author of the books *Lead with a Story*, *Sell with a Story*, and *Parenting with a Story*. He holds an MBA from the Wharton School, is a former consultant at Accenture, and former executive and twenty-year veteran of Procter & Gamble. He can be found at leadwithastory.com.

Appendix

Story Checklist

Use the columns on the following page to:

1. Prioritize your stories (A, B, C)

2. Note the name of the person or event you plan to craft the story about

3. Check off when you've finished crafting the story

Story #	Priority
Story 1: Where We Came From (A Founding Story)	0
Story 2: Why We Can't Stay Here (A Case-for-Change Story)	1
Story 3: Where We're Going (A Vision Story)	2
Story 4: How We're Going to Get There (A Strategy Story)	3
Story 5: What We Believe (A Corporate-Values Story)	7
Story 6: Who We Serve (A Customer Story)	4
Story 7: What We Do for Our Customers (A Sales Story)	5
Story 8: How We're Different from Our Competitors (A Marketing Story)	9
Story 9: Why I Lead the Way I Do (A Leadership-Philosophy Story)	6
Story 10: Why You Should Want to Work Here (A Recruiting Story)	10

Story	Done

Notes

i   Harvard psychologist Howard Gardner, as quoted in Richard Maxwell and Robert Dickman, *The Elements of Persuasion: Use Storytelling to Pitch Better, Sell Faster & Win More Business* (New York: HarperCollins, 2007).

ii   Gary Erickson, "Clif Bar: Gary Erickson," interview by Guy Raz, *How I Built This with Guy Raz*, NPR, January 1, 2018, https://www.npr.org/templates/transcript/transcript.php?storyId=572560919.

iii   "The Clif Bar & Company Story," Clif Bar & Company, accessed September 17, 2018, http://www.clifbar.com/article/the-clif-bar-and-company-story.

iv   Gary Erickson, *Raising the Bar: Integrity and Passion in Life and Business: The Story of Clif Bar Inc.* (New York: Jossey-Bass, 2004).

v   Erickson, "Clif Bar."

vi   Erickson, *Raising the Bar.*

vii   Constance L. Hays, "From Out of the Gym, Into the Grocery Store; Energy Bars Jump Into the Mainstream," *New York Times*, November 22, 1997. https://www.nytimes.com/1997/11/22/business/from-out-of-the-gym-into-the-grocery-store-energy-bars-jump-into-the-mainstream.html?pagewanted=all.

viii   Hayes Roth, "Apple, Disney, Facebook: Breakaway Brands Offer Simple Pleasures," *Forbes*, October 8, 2010, https://www.forbes.com/2010/10/08/google-facebook-disney-blackberry-apple-breakaway-brands-cmo-network.html#7fac2df20875.

ix   Amanda Aronczyk and Paige Cowett, "Son's Rare

Cancer Leads Family on Quest for Cure," NPR, February 9, 2015, https://www.npr.org/sections/health-shots/2015/02/09/383789122/sons-rare-cancer-leads-family-on-quest-for-cure.

x   "Please Grant 10-Year-Old Juntao (Joey) Xu Compassionate Use of Your Anti-PD-1/L1 Immunotherapy Drug," Change.org, https://www.change.org/p/merck-genentech-curetech-medimmune-lamberto-andreotti-sarah-koenig-carrie-fernandez-renzo-canetta-m-d-lisa-giezendanner-kenneth-c-frazier-gary-gilliland-eric-rubin-please-grant-10-year-old-juntao-joey-xu-compassionate-use-of-your-anti-pd-1-l1-immunot.

xi   Annette Simmons, *Whoever Tells the Best Story Wins: How to Use Your Own Stories to Communicate with Power and Impact* (New York: AMACOM, 2007), 99.

xii   Malcolm Gladwell, "How David Beats Goliath," *The New Yorker,* May 11, 2009.

xiii   John Pepper, *What Really Matters: Reflections on My Career at Procter & Gamble with Guiding Principles* for Success in the Marketplace and in Life (Cincinnati: Procter & Gamble, 2005), 181.

xiv Mark Satterfield, Unique Sales Stories: How to Get More Referrals, Differentiate Yourself from the Competition & Close More Sales Through the Power of Stories (Atlanta: Mandalay Press, 2010).

xv Paul Smith, Sell with a Story: How to Capture Attention, Build Trust, and Close the Sale (New York: AMACOM /Harper Collins, 2016).

xvi Ibid.

NEW! Only from Simple Truths®

spark impact in just one hour

IGNITE READS IS A NEW SERIES OF 1-HOUR READS WRITTEN BY WORLD-RENOWNED EXPERTS!

These captivating books will help you become the best version of yourself, allowing for new opportunities in your personal and professional life. Accelerate your career and expand your knowledge with these powerful books written on today's hottest ideas.

TRENDING BUSINESS AND PERSONAL GROWTH TOPICS

Read in an hour or less

Leading experts and authors

Bold design and captivating content